CW00621438

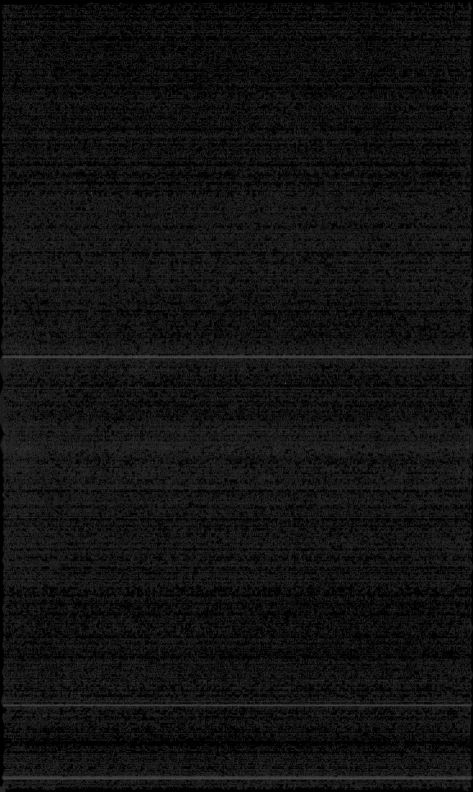

BLACK OVER RED

Also by Lotte Kramer

Ice-Break (Annakinn, 1980)
Family Arrivals (Poet & Printer, 1981 & 1992)
A Lifelong House (Hippopotamus Press, 1983)
The Shoemaker's Wife (Hippopotamus Press, 1987)
The Desecration of Trees (Hippopotamus Press, 1994)
Earthquake & Other Poems (Rockingham Press, 1994)
Selected & New Poems 1980-1997 (Rockingham Press, 1997)
Heimweh-Homesick, ed. Beate Hörr (Brandes & Apsel, 1999)
The Phantom Lane (Rockingham Press, 2000)

Lotte Kramer

Black over
Red

Rockingham Press

Published in 2005 by
The Rockingham Press
11 Musley Lane,
Ware, Herts SG12 7EN
www.rockinghampress.com

British Library Cataloguing-in-Publication Data

A catalogue record for this book
is available from the British Library

ISBN 1-904851-02-9

Printed in Great Britain
by Biddles Limited
King's Lynn

For Tessa
in gratitude

CONTENTS

Acknowledgements

With thanks to the editors where some of these poems first
appeared:

*Acumen, Agenda, Ambit, Candelabrum, Common Ground,
Country Life, The Countryman, Cambridgeshire Life,
Dreamcatcher, European Judaism, The Express, The
Hedgerow, Hearing Eye Anthology, Headland, Interpreter's
House, The Jewish Quarterly, The London Magazine,
Leviathon, Living Judaism, The Month, Other Poetry, Orbis,
Poetry Nottingham International, Poetry Express, The Rialto,
Scintilla, Second Light, Spokes, Stand Magazine, The Times,
Tribune* and *Ver Poets' Anthology.*

'Black Over Red' won Second Prize in the Manchester
Cathedral Competition; 'Exodus' won Third Prize in the
Second Light Competition and was a Poem on the Underground
in 2003.

Aspen Tree your leaves glance white into the dark.
My mother's hair was never white.

Paul Celan
(translated by Michael Hamburger)

Presentiment – is that long Shadow – on the Lawn
Indicative that Suns go down –

The notice to the startled Grass
That Darkness – is about to pass –

Emily Dickinson

THE PUPPETEER

He stands above them like a giant God,
A web of wires moves inside his hands

And gives them life. Some dance and sing or act out
Fairy tales that have a nightmare ring

With limbs as agile as a lizard's tongue.
One flops into a chair and folds his legs

In bored, superior attitude, his head
Right-angled, bent, full of world pain.

Grotesque or elegant, they populate
The stage with all our masks and weaknesses,

His creatures every one, and yet he hides
Behind this power game of wood and wire,

His life a shadow of their words and songs,
The Grand Guignol performing till his scene

Has ended in collapse. Then they are folded,
Bedded side by side in tissued trunks

And he stands empty in his fleshly frame,
His ordinary hands hang by his thighs.

MORNING

The swish of curtains
In the morning
Demands the day.
    Sun trying to emerge
    Through dirty windows
    Marbles the floor,

The heirloom room
With preferred shabbiness
From past histories.
    Worn textures fading
    Into our present
    With warm hands.
All greeting my daily
Experiment with the truth
And accident of living.

EXODUS

For all mothers in anguish
Pushing out their babies
In a small basket

To let the river cradle them
And kind hands find
And nurture them

Providing safety
In a hostile world:
Our constant gratitude.

As in this last century
The crowded trains
Taking us away from home

Became our baby baskets
Rattling to foreign parts
Our exodus from death.

FISH MARKET NOW AND THEN

He says he hates fish, never eats one bite,
But on the slab there lies his bread and butter,
The slithering fillets catching gems of light
With queuing women waiting for their supper.

He treats them royally, beheads, dissects
And skins and cleans, each order neatly
Executed, wrapped with chat and risky jokes
That warm with giggles their cold tired feet.

My weekly treat is ready when I come:
Pink tails of salmon, fresh as mountains streams.
Abroad I watched my mother point: "That one"
And it was hauled from tank where it would swim

And snuffed out with one blow on to its head –
She'd never buy a fish that had been dead.

A LETTUCE WITH HERBS

I was sent down the hill
To the greengrocer shop
To buy a lettuce with herbs

That smell of freshness
Of chives, borage, dill,
As electric then as now

As I cut those couriers
In my garden bed
Filling my senses

With currents of joy.
Their fragrance invites
That dusty street

12

Snaking down the hill
And I skipping up
With a bundle of greenness.

BAROMETER

Carved of brown Black Forest wood,
Ornate on our hall wall,
It is more intense than a weather chart
Consulted by him every morning.
A ritual initiation into the day's demands.

For years it has prophesied
The highs and lows of his life,
A net engulfing him,
Determining correct prognosis.
A strange drug he is addicted to
That hardly ever lets him off the hook.
He needs it like strong coffee each day.

THE CROSSING

Always the return:
To a home, a town,
A love, a mother's
Continuous embrace.

But there is only
Crossing of frontiers.

And in crossing is
Inevitable loss,
But also the gift
Of a new country,

After the sea's parting
And the password: need.

TO CROSS A BRIDGE

To cross a bridge.
Is walking to a new country.
The river in all its moods
A natural frontier
To savour in passing,
The bloodstream feeding both sides.

You imagine the foreign language,
Other sounds that will await you
With only a tinge, perhaps,
Of familiar evocations.

Sometimes you stand still
At the centre of the span,
In no-man's-land,
Gazing at new buildings
And altered landscapes,
Another world in transit.

NO RETURN

That house on the hill was not the house he knew.
Not his grandmother's house by the Vienna woods
where his early summers were spent and he grew
Into a young monkey climbing the roof, flat

In the Bauhaus style. Against the dictate
Of the family he would dance and sing
Up there, arias of operas, imitate
Wagner's long-winded hero, Wotan, the Ring.

Now, walking the tree-rich street to the hill
He was met by that Austrian rustic
Look, the white-washed extended base and walls,
The gabled roof, the last insult, a sick
Gemütlichkeit – and the forbidding face
Of the post-war owner shutting the door on us.

14

SOMETIMES

Sometimes
When I can cross the pain,
I find your azure certainty,
Your smiling gentleness:

Your shopping net
A careless balance
To the afternoon.
You meet my schoolday stream
With kneading hands of bread.

On other days
Your face is thin as gauze.
Your uncombed hair,
Your searching hands
Awake with fissured skin
Deforming loneliness to fear.

MY FATHER WAS A WRITER

My father was a writer.
His dusty manuscripts
Were stacked like paper patterns
In corners of his desk.

When young, his plays were living
On stages by the Rhine,
And promises of vision
Traced humour through his time.

I still remember photos:
Surrounded by his cast,
A minor Proust – and almost
A scalpel poised as sharp.

In Kaiser's war-time dodgings
He found Roumania's heat.
There, in a soldier's lodging
He daily stencilled sheets

With finely measured letters
Describing dirt and blood.
He bundled them like treasures
And kept the drawer shut.

"I'll write a tragedy one day"
He used to prophesy,
He never saw his Jericho
After the trumpet's cry.

QUICKSAND

There must have been
A waiting in the air,
A sort of dying
We know nothing of.
Not like a war,
A combat, a quick kill,
No tooth for tooth
But quicksand in the wind.

Some stood at praying
On Atonement Day
And swayed with vows:
'Kol Nidrei Adonai'
When that feared whisper crept
Below their chant
They dropped their prayer-shawl
And slowly went.

SAVED

My aunt survived the war in Southern France.
A camp inmate to be dispatched to death,
A case of interest for the medics there.

She suffered from a tumour on the brain.
So they decided on experiments
To operate her conscious and aware.

They tapped and poked the inside of her head
Until they found what they were looking for
And made her answer questions with each touch.

The nuns looked after her for many years
While husband, sister, disappeared for good
And she survived in bed, hole in her head.

After the war her brother found her there,
A wreck, and yet she gained in strength and lived
Determined to old age to tell her tale.

POST CARD
a boy speaks:

This empty post card in my hand
A gift from the Red Cross
On liberation from the camp.

I look at it, acutely sense
The loss and loneliness,
The brutal disappearances.

No echoes in my lanes and woods,
No sibling voices sing,
No table with my mother's food.

My childhood earth and alien wall,
My schooldays poisoned in their prime,
My orchard apples unpicked fall.

No one to receive a line,
My village foreign now,
My home no longer is my own.

WHERE

Where shall we walk to when the dust obscures
Hearing and sight, when bones and muscles fold
Away agilities and skin endures
The parchment heat of years? Shall blood run cold
Before heights are explored and stand revealed,
Where all the voices ever known return
Praising and weeping, where secrets once concealed
Assert themselves with newness and confirm:

'Yes, it was worth the snake-pass and the maze,
The water-logged and swampy fen that lost
Traces in mist.' So much we learned from days
That left us breathless, nights that grew and crossed
Our limbs with fire. But where's the path we dream
Will lead us painlessly, compel us home?

AT HOLY WELL EXCAVATION

Is this the meaning of autumn:
The leaves dying at their brightest,
A life ebbing at its peak,
The word struck dumb in its sentence,
The day's nerve sterile in darkness?

Ancient, this well
Lies opened out to the world,
Inside its new cave
Stand monastery walls,
Thick as mountains,

Touching air again.
Even the Roman stone,
Now naked and exposed,
Chips under the children's
Jumping feet.

Slowly, I return
To my modern house
Having seen answers
In a thread of water,
In a morning's minute.

UNDER THE STAIRS

Father, Mother, Son, Daughter-in-law,
We all crouched in a knot under the stairs
Waiting for sudden explosions, in awe
of eery calm after the shuddering house,

Hoping for the thin, shrill whine of all-clear
That would restore reluctant beds to us,
Thinking of nothingness, only the fear
Of this, our unchosen togetherness.

But still preferred to the outdoor shelter,
The cold damp cave of snoring nightmares,
Or else we could have ignored the danger
Of air-raids piercing our sleep, the flares

Of searchlights shocking the sky, rubble and heat
Somewhere other, selfishly, not in our street.

SUITCASE *

Grey and tattered it stands in the attic
Having accomplished sixty odd years
Of survival and childhood memories,
Stuffed tight with mother love and heartache,

Unable to forget the packed trains
Of ownerless children and platforms of tears
Its pock-marked skin a testimony
And emblem of such histories.

What now in this war-world of cul-de-sac lives,
Seekers of all ages for a place to own
Confronting friendlessness in a strange town,
A suitcase, perhaps, of unhappy souls

To be stored in some future eventual attic
Or dumped in a museum as showpiece of luck.

* *I refer to the suitcase I was allowed to take out
of Nazi Germany as a Kindertransport child*

EXPLAIN REVENGE

"Why did they bomb our village, what have we done?
My face is raining tears all day and night,
My husband and two children dead and gone."

She cannot understand this latest sign
Of terror language and the deed of hate:
"Why did they bomb our village, what have we done?"

The mutilation of her tiny world, the plan
To starve her people in their homeless plight,
"My husband and two children dead and gone."

20

Explain revenge for towers falling down,
For broken messages, love contact lost –
"Why did they bomb our village, what have we done?"

For bodies jumping, plunging under stone
Fire and dust, for creeds that cannot last –
"My husband and two children dead and gone."

We saw the view some years ago, had dinner, fun,
My New-York cousin proudly showed the sight.
"Why did they bomb our village, what have we done?
My husband and two children dead and gone."

TERROR

The tight silence
Of the upturned chair,
Legs in the air,
The unheard cry
Of the rush through the door,
Down the stairs,
Cup broken on floor,
A wound of tea,
The last look or plea
Before the cave
Of the van
Muddies the day
Or the bed of the ocean
Claims them.

note: written after having seen the opera
*   'The Lighthouse' by Peter Maxwell Davies*

TOWER

She likes to be alone as a rule
But not in here
Where dirty water drips from ceiling and walls
That have housed such terror
In past centuries.
This dungeon without light,
The rough stone floor,
The smell of vermin
Clutching the victim's throat
In his last hours,
A broken plank as bed
In this dark silence.

A sudden glimmer of light in a corner
Holds her eye,
She walks towards it with hesitation
And picks up a torn envelope
Discarded by a previous visitor
Containing a letter of rejection.
It brings her back to today's world
And the pain of living in it.
Someone has come to this place
To lose his humiliation here.

BOY

"I had no say in it.
They plucked me by the hair
Out of the crowd
And rushed me to the hospital.

I knew no one.
Had seen my father shot,
My mother beaten, chased away,

I ran and ran into the night
With shooting deafening the air

I found a cave to hide in,
Cold, alone, and slept a while.
At dawn I stumbled out
Looking for people, food,

And joined a group of children
Like myself, abandoned,
Wounded, stealing
Where we could
From empty houses.

The road was sandy, hot,
We swallowed dust and thirst,
But then it led us to the border
And to many hands."

PARADOX

The paradox of 'friendly fire'
Touches his smile
With cold fragility.

"My nephew died,
His mother's inconsolable."

Her doubled grief
Transmits a mutiny
To TV eyes and radio ears.

AFTER THE DISASTER IN JERUSALEM , THE BRIDE:

"Forgive me for my wedding day,
For dancing with such joy and bliss,
Forgive the floor-boards giving way,

The terror of the dark abyss,
The friends and lovers crushed to death,
The music stopping, all of this

Because the day was minted with
Our happiness that should endure
All tribulations of our earth.

Forgive, forgive, I can't say more
But never ever shall forget
That moment stays an open sore

For always, like our love, is caught
Between fulfilment and despair.
We must survive the blackest pit."

AN OLD PERSIAN RUG

Now getting threadbare, fringeless,
But still a fabled garden
With silky blue reflections
Telling of my father's shoes,
His driven restlessnes,
His huge mahogany desk,
His sacred study – a child's
Unbidden mystery
Surrounding him.

Packed in the bottom of my case
To cross the Channel with,
Under the necessary clothes,
The few belongings, photos
That were mine to take:
Some concrete souvenirs.
And it has travelled well,
Its beauty still intact
Caressing my eyes.

HOME TOWN IN WINTER

So I walked with you again,
This time in snow and rain
And wind that cut through bone.

Your cobbled streets and squares
Treacherous as grease
Yet precious too in ice.

You spoke of winter ways,
Of frosty hands and feet,
Escape to warmth, the glaze

Of tiles in walls, the stove
To hug and lean against
Affirming glow of life.

Sometimes I'd burn my hands
When touching that great hulk,
The kettle simmering in its hold.

I left you newly recognized,
The cold a balustrade
Draped now with beads of shades.

RHINELAND AUTUMN

I

Crossing the bridge, the mist
Had swallowed the Rhine
As we drove towards woods
Our fathers had loved to walk in.

Autumn had brushed its colours
On to leaves. Tree trunks,
Taller and straighter than remembered,
Were haloed by the idling sun.

All was silence and peace.
A Sunday morning prepared
With undiluted reverence
For the forest's innocence.

II

Yesterday a chapel on a hill
In the most idyllic landscape:
A monument for the war-dead,
The fallen, for this land?
Or for our fathers' right
To cherish this earth, these trees?
Denied to them when exile
Remained their only escape.

III

I walk among old street names
Childhood assertions, security
For a while. Roman landmarks,
French influences, all witness
My remembrance. Not perishable.

JEWISH BRIDE
(Rembrandt)

A promise lies between their hands
That barely touch. His is the sure
Possession, folding gentleness.
Hers in the fragile fingertips,
Submission, simple trust.

This moment, longer than a life,
Shows all the tender complement
In his protecting gaze. Her dark
And inward eyes are still and safe.
A vow without a word.

Theirs not the lovers' hurried spell
But hope and wealth in solid time.
And he, whose brush could say so much,
Knew human poverty and felt
The saliency of joy.

WOMAN AT THE WINDOW
Caspar David Friedrich, 1822

You want to cup the oval of her head,
The hair piled up and neatly pinned to it,
The ears exposed beside the nape of neck.

The sloping shoulders gathered in the sleeves,
High-waisted pleats fall down in gentleness
To shroud her body to the ankle's edge.

And so she leans against the window sill,
A longing gesture takes us out with her
Into the harbour, hardly visible.

Some uprights tell of masts in dove-grey light.
She dreams, perhaps, of distant other worlds
While slippers firmly tread the wooden floor.

BLACK OVER RED
(Rothko)

You move into the chapel of his colours,
Black over red,
And sense the slight manoeuvre
Of a black door
Trying to invade the deeper space.
A fragrance away
Another panel invites light
To come forward
Almost closing a shutter on the swing
Of self-knowledge.
But your eye is halted again and again
By the fear
Of discovery, of blackness
Assuming power
Over hidden whiteness reaching
Another world
Where the sacred is never static.

MATISSE,
CHAPEL OF THE ROSARY

We came from the noise
In the valley
To this language of silence.

His eloquent line
Takes us up to the light,
To the chapel in Vence,

To the ultimate brightness
The simple statement
Of black on white,

To the lightening glass
Of azure, green, yellow,
The signs of Provence

That give us music
As varied as life
In its creation

When shadows are changing
The whiteness
To colours of seasons.

EARLY SUNDAY MORNING
(Edward Hopper)

In this bright silence
Shadows are parallel rivers
Without source or sea
Cutting through clarity
Where green shops sit
Static as monuments,
Dark as caves.

It is early.
Behind the red facade
Windows are promises
Of net curtains, half-drawn
Yellow blinds letting in air
On yawns and unmade beds.

The sky's blue whitens
To a distance as we
Are caught for ever
Watching the likely
Dialogue between
A leaning carnival kiosk
And a military water hydrant.

DREAM TALES

At night
As dusk slinks along the street
Lamp-lit rooms
Open their faces to the world.
Spaces that
Normally are shrouded and closed
Suddenly
Become a surprise of light
And as darkness
Intensifies the ordinary suburb
Is conjured
Into a Magritte picture
Where people
Are mysteries in dream tales
And trees
The black transfigured watchmen
Confronting
Unexpected lives.

LONGTHORPE TOWER

We liked the solid tower,
Squat and gold,
A campanile older
Than the street, cathedral
Bound. A lead
Back to the monks' procession.

To see time in the clay well
Is to breathe.
To know grass had its living
Then and now,
Rounded with chant their voices
Filled the ground,

Sheared over torpid seasons.

Behind my polished window,
Metal-framed,
The centuries are waning,
Plain-song flows
Across in mordent rivers,
Plangent grows
A swaying snake of legions.

YOUTH MAKING A BASKET

Longthorpe Tower, mediaeval painting on West Wall

He sits there for ever
Lifting his delicate arm,
Mallet in hand,
To a half-finished round
Plaiting the reeds
On prepared gesso
For centuries.

Time has obscured
His face with dampness,
But there is precision,
The skill of experience
In his whole body,
Agile as bent grass
Ready to withstand the wind.

His legs are firmly planted
On brown earth,
His slippered feet
In rhythm to his hands
Moving with each knot.
He will not look up,
Is consumed utterly.

LOSING THE EARTH

Still earthbound
You sit caged in the drone
That moves you to take-off.

You shudder
And climb in spasms
Through a collage of clouds

Now airborne
You're level with sun-heights
Of nowhere – vanished

Your world
Of stones and rivers
Of hugging houses.

Your loss
Has unlocked your freedom,
Has doubled the moment.

UNDER THE CHANNEL

A prison with glass eyes
But no view
In a stillness
Of dark no man's land
Only punctured
By banal promises
Of movements
That don't come true.
Our thoughts ahead
Of missed connections
Of desolate stations
Of luxury beds
Of light and air.

BERLIN

The Serbo-Croat taxi driver
Dodges through traffic to the airport,
Politely asking if the music
(Classical) is disturbing.

Berlin behind us, surprisingly
Green and bright, even friendly.
My anti-Prussian prejudice
Has slowly subsided.

The city emerges from division
And war-wounds with bits of wall
Still standing but broken like coded
Alibis of the Secret Police.

Almost uncanny, the helpfulness
Of bus drivers, officials, shop-assistants
The new cupola of the Reichstag
Illuminates the whole surroundings

Where Max Liebermann lived,
Now a rebuilt handsome house.
He had his studio windows blacked-out
After witnessing the Nazi torchlight parade.

'Unter den Linden' spreads itself
Again in all its grandeur,
Only the coldness of the Fidelio
Production, the most glowing of operas,

Is jarring in the rebirth of this city,
With its restored golden Synagogue
Dome shining across the river
As the massive black Pietà weeps.

note:Max Liebermann was a painter, the Pietà a sculpture
by Käthe Kollwitz.

JEWISH MUSEUM, BERLIN, 2000 '

A zinc shell
Housing a history
Of terror
In its emptiness.
A giddiness
Of uneven ground
Propels you forward
In zig-zag light
Towards inevitable
Darkness.
A forest of stone
Pillars brings
Escape into air,
Into exile.

FRAUENKIRCHE, DRESDEN

The great dome of the church
Is reinvented in the centre of Dresden.

New stones marry old,
Some still blackened with fire and smoke,

United in a jigsaw
As craftsmen return the strength of walls

Beauty is rescued,
A cross from England as reconciliation

A black rock,
The half-polished altar sculpted by a Jew.

And by the river Elbe
The city's new bruise of a Synagogue.

AT THE ERICH KÄSTNER MUSEUM, DRESDEN

"Emil and the Detectives"
In all languages
Line the shelves
In this sunny suburb
Dreaming in a leafy garden.

A boy, you used to lounge here,
On the wall, watching life.
A long way from the Berlin days
You knew so well,
The half-world of tarts,
Clowns and bars,
Of night-clubs and cafés,
All feeding your bitter satire.

And boys chasing a crook,
You in tune with them,
With their thoughts and language,
Their innocent humour.
Your concern was mankind.

And then they burnt your books
You, a lone figure at the back
Of the crowd, watching.

35

OPTIONS

From above
The lake is an emerald mouth
Wedged between lips of cloud
On steaming mountains.

From above
The rooftops of Vienna loiter
Among polished steeples
That house pleading and prayer

From below
Mountains are dark embroidered
Arms of temptation
That promise achievement and sweat.

From below
Facades are splendour and power
Of stone and spirit
Determined by reason.

BRIEF OGRES

"A bad season," the woman said, gift shop
Brimming with knick-knacks, unsold, unwanted
China and table-mats. "A fatal drop
In visitors because summer so bad

And winter as well the weather too cold,
No electricity for two whole weeks
Because of heavy snow-falls, all the world
Packed up and left us to our lonely peaks."

Today, a sweltering August day, the heat
Hangs like a blanket from the sky and stings

Us on our climb into exhaustion, sweat,
Were black-dog shadows from the cable-cars fling

Themselves across the meadows without sound,
Brief ogres leaping like omens on the ground.

THE FACE OF THE GLACIER

There is this steady treck to the glacier.
All humanity on the move
Where silence should prevail.
They trip over boulders and grass
Up this steep long valley
Surrounded by watching mountains
Alive with animal cries,
Birds and sheep on narrow ledges,
The shepherd's decisive whistle.
Ahead, the grey tongue receding,
Each year a forshortened hope.
As we approach the ice, a cold wind
Strikes our skin, and now:
His whole face is revealed,
A drama of existence
In exposed beauty and ugliness.

WILDSTRUBEL

I

Watching his many crags
And treacherous gullies,
His white ice-fields
From the comfort of my balcony
With only rooftops at eye-level,
There is this everlasting awe
Connecting his grandeur
With our pedestrian frailties.
Though I would never try
To conquer his massive height,
The silence he projects
Seeps into meadows and stones,
Into skirting trees,
The birds still circle the air,
The brooks still hurry down,
Everything new and always.

II

There is no malice in the greenness
Of this valley.
Water and wood smells, cut grass
Dominates the air.
A snail sits on a stone embarking
On its slimy journey
While we struggle with underused legs
To cover the miles
To the waterfall – an end in itself
Or a beginning,
Climbing mountains where future
Is unimportant.

MATTERHORN, ZERMATT CEMETERY

Surely he must be
One of God's fingers

Declining us
For the millionth time.

A signal, a warning
Pointing at life.

> They came in 1863
> To this magnet of utter strength
>
> Three Oxford graduates,
> A parson from Lincolnshire,
>
> Now on their graves
> Are plastic flowers.

And still he waits
High above judgement

Demanding
New hostages

In his great solitude,
Spending desire and glory

CONCERN

The lonely women in the Swiss hotels,
Their hair immaculate, their clothes to date,
Their habits regularly timed by meals
Of those delicious morsels on their plates

When at their little virgin tables bent
The waiter hops around them with his chat
Fulfilling all requests and whims to please,
Hoping that when they leave here they will press

A fat note in his palm. The women mostly
Hobble with old age, use sticks to help their
Walks on easy paths, a solitary
Moving of their limbs in mountain air.

What will await them when they do return
To empty rooms, to echoless concern?

ST. MARY'S ALTAR BY TILMAN RIEMENSCHNEIDER, CREGLINGEN

I
His hands are angels
Singing to each other,
His knife carves legends
From the souls of saints,
Exposing all the earth
Can grow and carry
To reach the ultimate.

II
On this soft hill,
Inside the gothic chapel,
The lime-tree claims

A painter's light and shadow;
The pine-wood frame,
A reddish tone that spills
Exuberance – here,
Mathematical,
His blade retells the past,
Marries the present,
A future shadow breaks:
The farmer's miracle is shared *
Disciples praise and tender
The devil and the saint.

III
And as the setting darkens
The evening sun will touch
The Virgin's face, elect
The girl in the Madonna,
Let all the world's
Great surgeries be stilled
Inside a cup of light,

* a farmer found a Host here while ploughing, in 1384

IN SICILY

I
The full moon surprised and illuminated Etna,
A huge cone covered in snow.

It has sent a river of volcanic ash
Grotesquely fertile like black Fen soil.

Up in Taormina the pavements are charcoaled
With slippery substance reminding me

Of London smog sooting cupboards,
Rimming china with funereal bandages.

Here, in this island of myths, an eruption
Promotes the welding of its citizens of many histories

Who have to live under that fire-cloud
With all the unpredictable consequences and voices.

But the sea maintains the last word,
The repetitive backdrop to wars and invasions.

II
Strange, they name Etna a female,
A beauty spewing fire
With lava language of the universe,
A woman prisoner of her own fury.

III
The melody of his Sicilian voice
Glories in the Temple of Concordia.
The best preserved in this valley
Because spared by invading Christians
Who regarded it as non-religious
In their anti-pagan campaign.

You look into the depth and centre,
The gold lime-stone pillars
A frame for light and the sacred
Illuminating this green height.

THEN AND NOW

At Chesters Fort,
The rosy-cheeked attendant
Smiles: "Cold wind today".

The dead trees
At the bridge still crack and sway
Our twentieth century feet

Caress new grass,
The barracks, bathhouse, wall,
And all around the wide

Northumbrian sky,
The searching light throws
Golden patchwork on the hills

Where snaking stones,
So many sweaty hands explore,
Have Latin names.

MONSAL TRAIL
(for May)

Wildflowers up to our shoulders
Wallpaper the rocks on either side
As we walk once again that trail
Of the disused railway line.
Hills draw us along this morning
When perfection has been given
As a luxury in our shrinking world.

In the valley the derelict mill
Waits with hollow eyes
For another resurrection breathing
Blood and purpose into its walls again
Inside and beyond this landscape
Is the experience of the next step.

WATENDLATH

The word,
Warm and round,
Takes us over hills
Into rusty bracken
With slate underfoot
And sheep looking on,
Perplexed.

We puff and sweat to the height,
Are surrounded by
Silent giants
Under a neurotic sky.

Stories await us
Down in the tiny hamlet
On its green bottom
By the sedgy pond,
The river's busyness.

A low-stretched white house
Has crouched here for generations
Providing tea and cakes.
Behind it the hills
Are bandaged red-brown,
October's signature
In this assuring world.

RIVER INCANTATION

That you
Who are so docile and so calm
Should gnaw amazing chunks of bank
Fills me with awe.
Today
The sun reverberates the glass

44

Illuminating mud and stones
And all is still.
Is it
Persistence, hunger, even greed,
Enabling you with toothless gums
To hollow out,
Usurp
These mother-troves from rock and earth?
A thief – would be too harsh a word
Applied to you,
Rather
I'd call you Knife of Mercury,
Know you as constant Sibyl Sound,
Pulse at my side.

AFTER THE FLOOD
(Four Haikus)

After the flood
The impermanent island
Floats like a glass jewel.

The river has lost its way
Usurping the land
With its broad belly.

The sun cares little
For the destruction
But heightens the tragedy

While clouds build their
Gigantic castles
Only to disperse them again

BRIGHTON

Somewhere the year ends red
With teeming sores
But here the sea-weed rots
In blackening curls,
In inky contrast to those
Chalky walls
That tower huge and creased
At 'our own risk.'

The white sun rubs its lather
Into stone
Scrambling the sand with sea foam
As it moves,
Shaming the daylight shining
Into dusk.

OUR SHORT SEASON

This is the land of grasses,
Of wild wheat
Stroking its beard in the wind
That dislodges our summer.

The sun is a moody halo
Cupped round houses
For these two-day fiestas
That honey the taste of July.

A man pushes his mower
On the opposite lawn,
Defying wild flowers
That brave our short season.

LYING IN STATE

In Westminster Hall
The great hammer-beam roof,
Survives the death-watch beetle.
A Lying in State.

Our lives continue
Little holiday outings,
Take the boat down the Thames
To the white elegance of Greenwich,
The river a big empty mouth
Broadening each minute,
Learning a new language:
The loss of trade.

Lining the route
Warehouses stand large
And hollow like unused
Victorian hospitals,
No longer bulging
With cargoes from the sea,
No cranes bending down
Gratefully. The green slime
Of the river bank creeps
On shore where we read
Funeral names:
          'Free Trade Wharf,
          Metropolitan Wharf,
          Oliver's Wharf'
Another Lying in State.

SONG OF THE EARTH
(Mahler)

He took the Chinese words
To fuse, distil his theme

He, who was born between
The heart of Europe's hills.

He pledged a world to earth
Beyond his clay's distress;

And pleading for a friend's
Close hand, found his farewell:

In mountains, lakes of life,
From raging blood to seed,

From breathing bone to stone
Craving eternity.

HARPSICHORD QUARTET

Warm, with the cello's worship moaned the air,
Terse linked the violins their wedded tune
To the metallic vibrant harpsichord.

Precision vied with passion, statements swept
The church to wider gates of consciousness.
The lazy afternoon dissolved in sounds.

MASCOTS

I

Superstition
Has no space for me,
But some things
Become mascots
To travel with.

So here
A small silver pencil
Kept in my handbag,
Tarnished but still
Intact.

A present
From my father
When I was at school,
Too elegant then
In rough days,

Yet now
Much cherished,
Good to hold between
Arthritic fingers
Writing these words.

II

Stones
On my kitchen
Window sill,
Collected from
Memorable places.

One large
Spiky grey granite
From a mountain pass
On the glacier edge
Of amazement.

Most favourite
A small flat pebble
Shiny as glass
In silent eloquence
From Rilke's grave.

THREE THINGS

Three things
He cannot face to do
Since he's been left alone:

The daily cross-word
Puzzle that had kept him shrunk
In the square of his chair,

Smoke his cigar
And pipe to shroud himself
In muslin isolation,

Work at his stamp collection,
The pride and care he took
In its precise selection

Of subjects musical.
All she approved of
Though they led away from her.

Now barred,
No small print, footnote,
To explain his own astonishment

As if her breath
Had kidnapped all his hobbies
Into exile, into death.

LIBRARY MEN

Those library men
In deep conversation
With dailies and weeklies,
They sit there and gossip
To out-of-work shadows,
They chuckle, they grumble,
They brood in aloneness,
In tweeds and in denims
And a jury of books.

SPIRIT

You come to me at night
In my dreams,
Making coffee on the kitchen table.

'Too many doors in this house'
You said again
As you bumped into each in turn.

Your presence the usual delight
And assurance,
Something I lack in my waking hours.

Now that I cannot see the world
Through your eyes
I miss that extra dimension you gave it.

Why are you here so vividly,
A spirit only,
When morning intrudes and demands?

AFTER THE WAKE

We walk away from the wake
Huddled in our own pain,
Your presence all around us.

You always listened by looking
And would have been amused to watch
This conglomerate of family and friends

From different departments of your life,
All getting to know each other,
Being led by you through this grief,

This maze of apposite mourning.
Old rivals embracing, now safe,
No longer competing for your time,

Unable to grasp their loss.
And presiding, your only brother
Left from seven siblings,

Regal, a sad King Lear,
Donating his last praises
For you who was without equal:

Lover, brother, friend.

BY THE CLIFFS

By the cliffs
On this salt-washed path,
Littered with sea-weed and pebbles,
You walk with us.

We watch surreal landscapes
Of glacier rocks
As the tide goes out

52

Only to return with foam and fury.

We hear your praises
Of the astonishing horizon
Changing with colour and light
To another aspect

Of the constant world
Still housing your spirit
In water and wind
And its mysteries.

EX-INDIA, 1940s

Quite shabby-elegant, in khaki army
Cast-off clothes, still from his India years,
Retired now, he'd totter round the house
Inspecting black-out curtains for a pleat

Of light, or feeding, talking to the cats,
As lack of conversation made him odd.
Somewhere there had been a sharp intellect
Submitted though to discipline and drill.

He would, in winter, carry in one hand
A paraffin-stove from room to smallest room,
Sometimes as laughing stock for younger eyes.
Perhaps there was an ogre buried in his youth,

Fear of neglect or an outsider's stealth
And he would rave and shout for trivialities.
A hypochondriac, he cured himself
With Christian Science terminologies.

But when his wife lay prostrate on the floor
After a stroke, he closed the door –
He sat and prayed beside her day and night
And no one knew or came until too late.

ANTIGONE

Knowing your merciless end will deprive you of light,
Lawless you buried the brother and followed your heart;
Not a negation of love, but a walled-in content
Followed the dust that rebelled in your self-searching hands.

Only a legend, we say, but a courage we lack,
Trekking indifferent bequests on grub-ridden streets.

SPONSORED WALK

I walk in freedom for captives of conscience.
Their thoughts are censored, their bodies frail.
They're kept in prison in damp and darkness.

I stretch my legs in morning brightness.
I watch the river slink and curl.
I walk in freedom for captives of conscience.

The wind conducts the wild dance of grasses.
The jackboot has shrunk their space to a nail.
They're kept in prison in damp and darkness.

Above me the sky in autumn blueness.
The birds rehearsing their winter trail.
I walk in freedom for captives of conscience.

They would converse with water's silence,
With liberty's smell of air and soil.
They're kept in prison in damp and darkness.

Language and thought for us are precious.
Denied to them in their mental jail.
I walk in freedom for captives of conscience
They're kept in prison in damp and darkness.

54

THREE HAIKUS

I

You talk of dying
But there's a new child, love-laboured,
Here in its first night.

II

I saw the children
Under piles of brick, their faces
Washed in clouds of dust.

III

On his deathbed Goethe
Asked for a dish of soil, crumbs
Of reality.

SESTINA

Writing a Sestina is quite defeating me.
I can see no point or purpose in it at all,
The artifice required does not satisfy
The making of a poem, the urgency
Of harnessing a thought like a horse
Is quite obliterated by mechanics.

I like the freedom of flow without mechanics,
The positioning of words alone is not for me
However beautiful and strong the horse,
However statuesque it shows it all
The lack is there without the urgency
And sentences no longer satisfy.

How can a well of stories satisfy
If it is strangled by such strict mechanics,
How can a river keep its urgency
And wander sideways in escaping me

Into some swamp or delta where it all
Evaporates together with the horse.

A train meanders past a field, the horse
Is grazing there, it seems to satisfy
The primitive, the animal instincts all,
Simplicity without the wrought mechanics.
This view from the train window pleases me
And underlines the quiet urgency.

Now in a Sonnet I can write with urgency,
Those fourteen lines are structured like a horse
Trotting along with ease to carry me
Via the stanzas that must satisfy
But not display the obvious mechanics,
The couplet at the end will clinch it all.

Or in that other discipline it all
Is featured, skill and urgency
Without concocting hair-splitting mechanics:
The Villanelle is like a well-trained horse
Performing its triangular dance to satisfy,
To hammer home its short refrain for me.

So tell me, all this tedious urgency,
A horse in harness will it satisfy
Life's rhythm with confined mechanics?

POSITIVE

To think, this autumn
Has contained all summer,

That summer took last winter
By the throat and stifled

Its fierce breath,

Our lives, like Russian dolls

Are present in this day,
In future's imminence.

I tear up sheets of words
Fragmenting thoughts

That grew and spilled themselves
In seeds of next year's spring.

RETREAT

In the autumn of my garden
Leaves are slowly losing their trees,
Mist is crouching between yesterday
And today, spreading its damp veil.

Flowers no longer splash their blood-spots
On to earth but curdle and retreat.
Only greenness asserts a facade
At the receiving end of the season.

LATE

Life
Has its pinacles still
Though more elusive
And rare now, more
Cumbersome to reach.
Reward will follow
For a short while only,
So I tell myself
At the basement door,
Locked.

SALT

Am I
Like Lot's wife
Having looked at Sodom
Now silenced
To a salt pillar
Without words?

My ghosts return
Unforgotten.

DISCARDED POEMS

They sit there
With their long necks,
Their drooping heads,
Their restless eyelids,
Waiting for the corset
Of card and print
To give them stability,
To be uprights in a vertical world.

True, they have had shelter
In papers and journals
Among illustrious company;
They have been voiced on airwaves
By well-meaning strangers;
But still they are longing
For sole fulfilment
Between named covers.

EVE TO ADAM

Sometimes we try
To rush against the Dark Thing,
Crush its potency,

Deflect its eye,
So that in blindness it should
Shudder on the ground
And leave us unprotected
In the whitest light.

So recognised,
As you in me and I in you,
The Dark Thing bleeds,
Or so it seems
As edges crumble
And we cave into
All future nights,
All Eden petrified.

TRIANGLES

At dusk on the edge of a month,
Only the solid moon hangs on
Divided light. In the forest

It is night already; and here,
On the long tarmac, the track splits
Its salamander skin. Distance

Narrows and ends under a hill's
Waist. Like a cancer the slow dull
Shadow contaminates each house

And only the occasional
Window measures a small, bright square.
Soon, a uniform indulgence

Will camouflage the last darkness,
And all the day's red triangles
Will fall – as charred fingers of straw.

LOOKING AND SEEING

I look into the leaves
And see them breathe
With early greenness.

Cowslip*, a key to earth,
A tiny parasol
Unlocking light.

The unmown meadow
A spun shawl of tall grasses
Singing with dandelions.

A cat sits still
On the tarmac, blinking
His search-light eyes.

In the museum, the angel
Spreads his wings
With mediaeval sight,

A carved tranquility
That tells of solitude
As privilege.

* *Schlüsselblume (German: "keyflower")*

Versions and Translations

THE PRISONER

(after Rainer Maria Rilke)

I

My hand has only one
gesture left to banish with;
dampness is falling from rocks
onto these old stones.

I hear only this knocking,
and my heart is in step
with the dripping movement
and melting with it.

Might drops fall faster
would an animal come again.
Somewhere else was brighter –
but what do we know then.

II

Think, what is now sky and wind,
air for your mouth and light for your eye,
it would become stone round the small space
where your heart and your hands are found.

And what you now call tomorrow and: then
and: later and next year and so on –
that would become a wound in you full of pus
and ulcerate never to break.

And that which has been would be insane
and raves inside you, the precious mouth
which never laughed now foaming with laughter.

And that which was God now only your guard
spitefully stuffing his dirty eye
into the last hole. And yet you are alive.

WOMAN LOSING HER SIGHT
(Rainer Maria Rilke)

She sat like all the others there at tea.
At first I felt she had a different way
of picking up her cup and once she smiled,
it almost hurt, she seemed to say.

And when at last they got up talking
and slowly wandered as by accident
through many rooms (talking and laughing)
I saw her then. She followed where they went.

Held back like one who must be singing
soon in front of many people
there was a brightness on her eyes
like on a pond from outside, pleasing.

She followed slowly and she needed time
as if to bridge a waiting handicap
and yet: once she had overcome the obstacle
she'd not be walking ever but be flying.

ALONE
(Herman Hesse)

Many roads and paths
Are leading across the earth
But all have the same end.

You can ride and travel
Two of you or three,
But the last step
You have to go alone.

No knowledge,
Nor ableness is as good
As tackling all difficulties
Quite alone.

63

SONG OF THE DEPARTED

after Georg Trakl

Full of harmonies is the flight of birds. At evening
The green woods have gathered into quieter huts;
The crystalline pastures of deer.
The dark calms the plashing brooks, the damp shadows
And the flowers of summer that peal with grace in the wind
Already there is dusk on the brow of musing men.
And a small lamp is shining, goodness in its heart
And the peace of a meal; for bread and wine
Are made holy by God's hands, and quietly the brother
Is looking at you with night-eyes, so that
He might be at rest from thorny wandering.
O to live in the soulful blueness of night.
Lovingly, too, the room's silence is embracing the old shadows,
The purple torments, lament of a great generation
That now walks piously in the solitary grandson.
For always from black minutes of madness the patient one
Awakes more radiant at the stony threshold,
And is powerfully surrounded by the cool blueness and shining
fall of autumn,
The silent house and the legends of woods,
Measure and law and the moon-touched paths of the departed.